D1212722

EDGE
BOOKS

WILD ABOUT SNAKES

CORN SNAKES

BY MELANIE A. HOWARD

Consultants:
Joe Maierhauser, President/CEO
Terry Phillip, Curator of Reptiles
Reptile Gardens
Rapid City, South Dakota

Edge Books are published by Capstone Press,
151 Good Counsel Drive, P.O. Box 669, Mankato, Minnesota 56002.
www.capstonepub.com

Books published by Capstone Press are manufactured with paper
containing at least 10 percent post-consumer waste.

Library of Congress Cataloging-in-Publication Data
Howard, Melanie A.
  Corn snakes / by Melanie A. Howard.
    p. cm. — (Edge books: wild about snakes)
  Includes bibliographical references and index.
  ISBN 978-1-4296-7664-9 (library binding)
  ISBN 978-1-4296-8018-9 (paperback)
  1. Corn snake—Juvenile literature. I. Title.
  QL666.O636H69 2012
  597.96'2—dc23   2011021020

Editorial Credits
Brenda Haugen, editor; Gene Bentdahl, designer;
   Laura Manthe, production specialist

Photo Credits
Alamy: Ian Watt, 13, Juniors Bildarchiv, 11, 26-27; AnimalsAnimals: Leszczynski,
Zigmund, 18; Corbis: Joe McDonald, 29; Dreamstime: Dave Mcnaught, 8, Erllre,
cover, Stanko Mravljak, 1; Getty Images: Oxford Scientific/John Mitchell, 14-15,
Science Faction/Fred Hirschmann, 9, Stone+/Chris Windsor, 25; The Kobal
Collection: New Line/James Dittiger, 4; Photolibrary: Peter Arnold Images/John
R. MacGregor, 17; photoshot holdings: Bruce Coleman/Kerry T. Givens, 22-23;
Shutterstock: D. Kucharski & K. Kucharska, 11, Eric Isselée, 11, erllre74, 7,
Kassia Halteman, 20-21

Artistic Effects
Shutterstock: Marilyn Volan

TABLE OF CONTENTS

LIGHTS, CAMERA, ACTION!

The plane shook. Oxygen masks fell from overhead. Along with the masks, so did snakes!

"Cut!" the director yelled.

The actors stopped pretending to be scared of the harmless snakes around them. Some even helped pass the snakes from the set to the **handlers**. It was time to switch the snakes for new ones. About 450 snakes were used for the movie *Snakes on a Plane*. But only 60 real snakes were on the set at a time.

Corn snakes were among the slithering **reptiles**. Their striking colors, great climbing skills, and comfort with people make them a popular choice to use in movies.

handler—a person who trains or manages snakes for work

reptile—a cold-blooded animal that breathes air and has a backbone; most reptiles lay eggs and have scaly skin

Popular Pets

Corn snakes are one of the most popular pet snakes in the United States. Because of the work of **breeders**, corn snakes come in more than 30 different color and pattern combinations.

In the wild, corn snakes are mainly found in the eastern United States from New Jersey to Florida. One type of corn snake, the Great Plains rat snake, lives as far west as Utah. But because snakes are good escape artists and popular pets, it's possible you might spot one outside its **range**. You might even find one in another country.

Corn Snake Range

☐ where corn snakes live

North America · Europe · Asia · Africa · South America · Australia · Antarctica

N W E S

breeder–a person who raises animals to sell

range–geographic region where an animal or plant species naturally lives

Great Plains Rat Snakes

The Great Plains rat snake is found mainly in Nebraska and Colorado. It is darker than most other corn snakes. It also is smaller than most other corn snakes. The Great Plains rat snake is rarely longer than 54 inches (137 centimeters). Other types of corn snakes can grow to 6 feet (1.8 meters) long.

The Great Plains rat snake lives in canyons and on hillsides. In drier areas, it usually lives near a spring, a place where water rises from underground.

spear-point pattern

What makes corn snakes frightening enough to use in scary movies? Corn snakes look like poisonous copperheads. Copperheads and corn snakes even live in some of the same places. Corn snakes sometimes get killed because people are afraid they have found a copperhead.

Like a copperhead, corn snakes are often red, brown, or tan. Corn snakes and copperheads also have similar saddle-shaped markings along their bodies. But there are several ways a corn snake is different from a copperhead.

First, a corn snake has a spear-point pattern on the top of its head. A copperhead doesn't have this pattern. A corn snake also has eyes with round **pupils**. A copperhead has slit-shaped pupils. And a corn snake does not have heat-sensing pits or **venom** like copperheads do.

copperhead

pupil—the round, dark center of the eye that lets in light

venom—a poisonous liquid produced by some animal

Spotting a Corn Snake

Corn snakes come in a wide variety of colors. Some are red or tan. Others may be yellow, orange, or gray. In **captivity**, corn snakes come in colors not usually found in the wild. One example is a color breeders call snow, which is mostly white.

Many corn snakes' tails have two dark stripes underneath them. Some corn snakes have a checkerboard pattern on their bellies. Many corn snakes have black edges on their markings, but others don't. With the wide variety of corn snake colors and patterns, it's easy to see why they are hard to identify. The one thing all corn snakes have is the spear-point pattern on their head. But that pattern can be hard to see depending on a snake's coloring.

Breeders' Paradise

Corn snakes make wonderful pets. They come in a wide variety of colors and patterns. A breeder can get a striped or a spotted snake when breeding corn snakes. Or neither! A type of corn snake called blizzard appears completely white, often whiter than a snow corn snake. Any pattern on a blizzard corn snake's body is so faint that it appears to have no pattern at all. Other popular corn snakes include the reverse okeetee, bloodred stripe, charcoal, and lavender. The okeetee corn snake in the pet trade is the classic corn snake. It has black-edged saddle markings on its body. A reverse okeetee corn snake has white-edged saddle markings. A bloodred stripe corn snake has a deep red body and stripes rather than saddle markings. It has little or no black markings in its pattern. A charcoal corn snake has no red in its markings. It has a gray body with darker saddle markings. A lavender corn snake looks much like a charcoal corn snake. But the lavender corn snake's background color makes the snake look purple.

On the Defensive

Being mistaken for a copperhead may not always be good for corn snakes. But that does not stop them from pretending to be dangerous snakes when they are threatened. Like a copperhead, a corn snake vibrates its tail against dry leaves or twigs to make a threatening sound when it senses danger. Corn snakes and copperheads do not have rattles like rattlesnakes do. But corn snakes and copperheads thrash their tails around, making enough noise to scare off other animals. Corn snakes may also **strike** repeatedly at an enemy.

A corn snake may use body bridging to scare off its enemies too. When body bridging, the snake raises the front of its body in a line **horizontal** to the ground. This positioning makes the snake look bigger than it really is.

corn snake body bridging

What's in a Name?

Some experts believe corn snakes got their name because their body patterns look like Indian corn. Indian corn has a spotted pattern much like the belly of a corn snake. Others say corn snakes got their name from where farmers often found them— in their corn cribs.

Rodents in search of food often go into places where farmers store corn and grain. Corn snakes go into these storage areas to hunt the rodents, which makes the snakes helpful to farmers.

rodent—a mammal with long front teeth used for gnawing; rats, mice, and squirrels are rodents

habitat—the natural place and conditions in which an animal or plant lives

Hunting Habits

Corn snakes are shy in the wild. They prefer to hunt at night or early evening. Corn snakes often hide and rest during the day. Some of their favorite hiding spots are under rocks and logs and underground. Since rodents often make their homes underground, corn snakes will hunt them there as well.

Corn snakes live just about anywhere they can find food. They can be found in prairies, woodlands, and other **habitats**. They may live in trash piles, barns, and in the rafters of houses. Corn snakes have adapted well to human environments.

Corn snakes also eat frogs, lizards, and bats. They will climb trees to hunt birds and will eat birds' eggs too.

Chapter 3

COLORFUL CONSTRICTORS

How does a corn snake kill without venom? Corn snakes are **constrictors**. They don't belong to the same family as boa constrictors or other well-known constrictors. But they kill their **prey** the same way—they squeeze it to death.

A corn snake lies in wait and then ambushes its prey. The snake bites its prey and holds it in its jaws to keep it from running away. Then the snake wraps its body around the prey. A corn snake uses its powerful muscles to squeeze until the prey stops breathing. If the prey is very small, a corn snake might swallow it alive. But usually the snake swallows its prey headfirst after the animal is dead.

A corn snake doesn't need to eat every day. It may go days or weeks without eating, depending on how big its last meal was.

Corn snakes are more active when they are hungry. Changes in air pressure and temperature that happen before a storm also make a corn snake more energetic.

constrictor–a type of snake that wraps around its prey and squeezes

prey–an animal hunted by another animal for food

Mating and Reproduction

Wild corn snakes mate in spring. Male corn snakes compete for females. The males may lunge at each other or try to pin the other snake to the ground. The winner earns the right to mate with the female.

In summer, female corn snakes may lay more than 30 eggs at a time. Often the eggs are laid in a rotting stump or on dying plants. Places where plants or trees are breaking down and rotting create heat and humidity. The rotting plants help keep the eggs at the perfect temperature, which is about 82 degrees Fahrenheit (28 degrees Celsius). After laying the eggs, the female's work is done.

A two-headed corn snake once lived at the San Diego Zoo. Its name was Thelma and Louise. Before it died, Thelma and Louise had 15 normal corn snake young.

Hatchling Growth

Corn snake **hatchlings** are not as boldly colored as are adults. Newly hatched corn snakes are between 8 and 12 inches (20 and 30 cm) long. Young corn snakes often feed on frogs, lizards, and baby mice until they are big enough to tackle larger prey. A corn snake may be several months old before it starts eating adult rodents.

A corn snake reaches adulthood between 18 and 36 months. A fully-grown corn snake is usually between 3 and 5 feet (0.9 and 1.5 m) long. How big a corn snake grows depends on what it can find to eat in the wild. A well-fed corn snake might be 6 feet (1.8 m) long.

The average height of an American male is 5 feet, 10 inches (178 centimeters).

hatchling—a recently hatched animal

predator—an animal that hunts other animals for food

Most corn snakes don't reach adulthood because **predators** such as large birds eat baby corn snakes.

Shedding

As a corn snake grows, it sheds its skin. A new layer of skin forms under the old layer. A snake sheds its outer skin all at once. If a corn snake sheds its skin in pieces, it may be a sign that the snake is sick.

A corn snake will also shed its skin if it gets injured. Severe injuries may lead the snake to shed more than once.

Female snakes often shed right before laying eggs. They often shed after laying eggs as well.

Chapter 4

CORN SNAKES AS PETS

Corn snakes make great pets. They have a gentle nature and come in a variety of colors. They don't have as many special needs as other snakes. But it's best to buy a corn snake soon after it's born so it gets used to you right away.

Before getting a corn snake, however, there are some things to keep in mind. A corn snake can live more than 20 years in captivity. It will also require enough space to move around comfortably and grow.

Also, keep in mind that snakes can bite. Corn snakes are usually calm when held. But like all snakes, they are unpredictable. Corn snakes may be more likely to bite around the times they shed. A corn snake bite can be painful.

Choosing Your Pet

You can get a pet snake from a breeder or a pet store. Try to make sure the pet is not from the wild. A snake born in captivity is likely to be friendlier toward people. It's also less likely to carry diseases. Making sure pet snakes are not taken from the wild also helps the wild corn snake population stay strong.

Talking to a reptile expert at a pet store, university, or other organization before getting a pet snake is always a good idea. They will have good information about how to care for a pet snake.

Dangers in the Wild

Wild corn snakes face more dangers than pet corn snakes do. Wild snakes are often exposed to parasites and germs. A wild snake can get sick from drinking unclean water or eating infected food.

Mites and ticks are parasites that will latch onto a snake and drink its blood. A mite could spend its whole life feeding off one snake. This can make the snake sick. Mites and ticks sometimes cause blood infections that can make the snake anemic. When a snake is anemic, it doesn't have enough blood to function normally.

Coexisting

Corn snakes still thrive in the wild in most areas. But Florida and New Jersey have both listed corn snakes as **protected**. In both of these states, habitat loss has threatened the snakes' survival.

People must respect corn snakes if the snakes are to continue to thrive. Don't make a wild corn snake a pet. Always call officials to have a snake taken away rather than killing it. Snakes play an important role in nature. They kill rodents that carry diseases that can make people sick. Without snakes, diseases could spread more easily.

Corn snakes are beautiful, adaptable creatures. We can learn to adapt to them too.

protected–defended against dying out

GLOSSARY

breeder (BREED-ur)—a person who raises animals to sell

captivity (kap-TIV-ih-tee)—the condition of being kept in a cage

constrictor (kuhn-STRIK-tur)—a type of snake that wraps around its prey and squeezes

habitat (HAB-uh-tat)—the natural place and conditions in which an animal or plant lives

handler (HAND-lur)—a person who trains or manages snakes for work

hatchling (HACH-ling)—a recently hatched animal

horizontal (hor-uh-ZON-tuhl)—flat and parallel to the ground

predator (PRED-uh-tur)—an animal that hunts other animals for food

prey (PRAY)—an animal hunted by another animal for food

protected (proh-TEK-ted)—defended against dying out

pupil (PYOO-puhl)—the round, dark center of the eye that lets in light

range (RAYNJ)—geographic region where an animal or plant species naturally lives

reptile (REP-tile)—a cold-blooded animal that breathes air and has a backbone; most reptiles lay eggs and have scaly skin

rodent (ROHD-uhnt)—a mammal with long front teeth used for gnawing; rats, mice, and squirrels are rodents

strike (STRIKE)—to hit or attack someone or something

venom (VEN-uhm)—a poisonous liquid produced by some animals

READ MORE

Case, Russ. *Snakes*. Beginning Vivarium Systems. Irvine, Calif.: Advanced Vivarium Systems, 2007.

Craats, Rennay. *My Pet Snake*. My Pet. New York: Weigl Publishers, 2011.

Howard, Melanie A. *Copperheads*. Wild about Snakes. Mankato, Minn.: Capstone Press, 2012.

INTERNET SITES

FactHound offers a safe, fun way to find Internet sites related to this book. All of the sites on FactHound have been researched by our staff.

Here's all you do:

Visit *www.facthound.com*

Type in this code: 9781429676649

INDEX